Great Hunters

Trophy Room of Stuart Edward White

Their trophy rooms & collections

Safari Press Inc.

Acknowledgment of Photographers

1. James & Laurie Bibler/Steve Newby Photo Studio
2. Roger R. Card/Ferris State University, Bill Bitzinger
3. Stephen Dean/Richard's Photography, Tallahassee, Florida
4. Soudy Golabchi/Brian Robins Photography
5. Jacques and Micheline Henrijean/Tennants Auctioneers
6. Bela Hidvegi/Tibor Papp
7. Dr. J. Y. Jones/Bill Thomas
8. Fred Koken/Donald E. Manzer & Art Sutch
9. Rudolf and Cordelia Kräling/Peter Dorn
10. Dr. James J. Lapinsky/A. Michael Lucas Photography
11. Gib Lewis /Perry Langenstein, with International Theatre Consultants
12. Harald Müller/Willie Oosthuizen
13. Miguel Nuñez/Pau Golano
14. Sam & Rosemary Pancotto/ Robert Anderson photo library
15. Richard Pierce/Chip Hollister
16. Walt Prothero /Walt Prothero
17. Gary & Yvonne Rigotti/Isaac Whitlatch/ Jared Cruce Photography
18. José M. Sodiro /Fito Previderé
19. Dr. Adrian de Villiers/Chris Townsend
20. Jesús Yurén/Rafael Corrales

First edition

Safari Press

2011, Long Beach, California

ISBN 978-1-57157-356-8

Library of Congress Catalog Card Number: 97067705

10 9 8 7 6 5 4 3 2 1

Printed in China

Readers wishing to receive the Safari Press catalog, featuring many fine books on big-game hunting, wingshooting, and sporting firearms, should write to Safari Press, P.O. Box 3095, Long Beach, CA 90803, USA. Tel: (714) 894-9080 or visit our Web site at www.safaripress.com.

TABLE OF CONTENTS

Hunters listed alphabetically

The Trophy Room

Trophy rooms are as individual as the men who create them. The trophy room is a visual list of a man's aspirations, experiences, and accomplishments throughout his lifetime of hunting. In each of these rooms you will see the progress of a hunter as he goes from a boy or young man with little hunting experience to a fully mature person with dozens, and sometimes hundreds, of hunting trips to his name.

These trophies and photographs represent the excitement, adventure, challenges, and victories of the hunt. They are a visual memory of the new places the hunter explored and the people he worked with on all his trips. They recall the professional hunters and trackers who made sure each trip was successful, and they represent the bonds of friendship with these people.

When you look at these trophy rooms, you'll see that hunting is about working hard, setting goals, and following through. It's about the great stories that are shared around the campfires and the plans for the next hunt. Each trophy room tells a story about the hunter's life, and it is the place where the hunter shares those hunts and the warmth of his fireplace with his friends and family. It is the place where the hunter dreams about his future expeditions. While some may only see a room full of hairy creatures that collect dust, we hunters see a room that brings back memories from the frozen north, the highest peaks, the swamps, the brush country, and the deserts of the world. Each trophy and each trophy room has the power to evoke wonderful memories of the experiences we've had.

Here, in these pages, are the finest trophy rooms in existence; they are rooms without peer, from the world's hunting elite. These rooms are to be enjoyed by all who open the pages of this book. It is our hope that this book will inspire hunters everywhere to plan their own next trip while giving them ideas about how to design or expand their own trophy rooms. The contributors of this book had a great desire to reach the summits of their sport, and these pages will offer a glimpse into the hunting done by these people. ***Great Hunters 6*** *is a visual celebration of the trophy room, one of the oldest expressions of mankind.*

Frank J. Zitz
Frank J. Zitz & Company
Rhinebeck, New York
June 2010

BIBLER

I grew up an avid outdoorsman enjoying all types of hunting and fishing. I was born and raised in Scottsville, Arkansas, where my grandfather started the family business, Bibler Bros. Lumber Company, an enterprise that I have the privilege now to own and carry forward. My love for hunting started when I was twelve. My uncles—Burl, Dean, and Ewing Bibler—would take me bird hunting on the weekends, and to impress the importance of safety to me, they would give me only one shell at a time for my borrowed 12-gauge, double-barrel shotgun, which weighed about as much as I did. If not expended, they would take shell back.

Once I ventured out of the beautiful state of Arkansas, my desire to hunt also exploded. As the years went by, it was as if I just couldn't get enough; I wanted to experience hunting not only all over the western states, but I was also curious about what Africa and other countries might have to offer. It wasn't until the spring of 1999 that I was finally able to realize my lifelong dream of hunting around the world. My first trip abroad was to South Africa, and I was amazed at the diversity of animals and their habitats. I was successful in harvesting approximately sixteen animals—a great beginning for a trophy room that was then only in my imagination.

We made an addition to an existing detached recreation room for my first trophy room. Although we referred to it as the "barn," it was a long way from being a barn. By the time the barn was completed, I had over thirty animals waiting to be housed. After obtaining over seventy trophies, my barn was totally destroyed by fire in February 2005. While devastating to us, it certainly wasn't a deterrent to my hunting. If anything, it just increased my momentum. I not only got in high gear to re-create a bigger and better "trophy house," I doubled up on my hunting. Within the first two years after the fire, I had rebuilt it from the ground up.

My wife, myself, and a good friend and well-known architect, David Johnston, from Aspen, Colorado, designed my new trophy house. Herb Millsaps was the lead contractor and Gordon Higgs supervised, both longtime friends. A local craftsman, Lyle Ratzlaff, built the extraordinary cabinetry and the exquisite door. Without these craftsmen and their employees, we would not have this beautiful structure to display my trophies.

The pursuit of exotic animals has taken me and sometimes my wife to South Africa twice, Tanzania, Botswana twice, Zambia, the Central African Republic, Namibia, Ethiopia, Cameroon, Mongolia, Mexico, New Zealand, Australia, and Spain.

James & Laurie Bibler

CARD

When I was asked to write a few words about what my trophy room means to me, it was a moving experience to put my feelings into words. All hunters share a reverence for the animals they have taken. It is impossible to view a trophy and not recall all the details of a particular hunt. The Card Wildlife Educational Center has over 180 species, and when I look at any one of them I conjure up memories of each experience. Most importantly, each species represents an adventure. It is the fellowship of hundreds of people—professional hunters, guides, trackers, outfitters, camp staff, travel agents, and hunting buddies who have all played a part in these endeavors—that brings the fondest memories. Very few of the trophies were a solo endeavor. Most were a team effort, and I just happened to be the captain.

Card Wildlife Educational Center

My first trophy room started out as an office in my construction company. It became such a popular destination for Boy Scouts, Girl Scouts, church groups, and school field trips that sometimes I wondered if it really was a business office. One day while I was in a meeting about an addition to a building at my alma mater, Ferris State University in Big Rapids, Michigan, someone asked about putting a full-mounted bear in the lobby. From that simple inquiry, the seed was planted for the entire project.

Today the center occupies 5,000 square feet of the Arts and Science building, and we are extremely proud to host over 9,000 visitors annually. Most of these people have no idea who I am. They simply come for the experience of seeing this vast collection of animals from around the world. To share my collection with the public in this manner has given me more satisfaction than I ever dreamed possible. These mounts are the accumulation of a lifetime dedicated to the pursuit of big-game hunting, and I just love hearing a third grader gasp in excitement at the size of a lion or the ugliness of a warthog. My last few years have been dedicated to adding specific animals that the children will love to see. "Roger Card, the big-game hunter" has made an effort to collect a capybara, ostrich, African porcupine, 400-pound black marlin, and several other trophies just to add to the delight of visiting children.

I truly enjoyed each minute of every hunt while collecting these trophies, but putting them in the Card Wildlife Center and sharing them with future generations has been the most fulfilling part of my hunting passion. I never saw it coming, but when I reflect on my proudest moments as a hunter, seeing the wonder in visitors' eyes as they tour the center, repeatedly takes first place. I cannot think of a better purpose for a big-game trophy collection.

Blue Wildebeest
Blesbok

DEAN

I did not grow up with a rifle and fishing rod in my hand. It was only when I was in law school that I was introduced to fishing and duck hunting. I totally lacked the patience for fishing, but I loved duck hunting. Deer hunting was a natural progression from duck hunting, but I found that to be successful with deer requires the hunter to have a job that permits him time to stay in the woods. I either had to change jobs or my method. In the summer of 1995, I called up a hunting outfitter about a fall deer hunt for my brother, Greg, and me. His clients were totally booked, but, in an exchange that would change my life, the agent said he could fix us up with a hunt in Africa in spring.

"You clearly have me confused with someone who has money!" I replied.

He laughed and explained that we could hunt in the Republic of South Africa (RSA) for ten days for eight animals for less money than the cost of a deer hunt out West. I was sold, and selling my brother proved even easier because he had less time to hunt than I.

We hunted with Chappie Scott, one of the founders of the safari business in RSA. Our hunt in the mountains of the Eastern Cape was unforgettable. Looking around at the six inches of snow that covered the land, we kept repeating to ourselves, "Can you believe this is AFRICA?" The friendliness of the South Africans was another surprise, as was their hardiness, which can best be summed up by mentioning the great **braai** *(BBQ) we had outdoors—in driving snow! With Ashley King, our professional hunter, my brother and I took twelve animals between us. That was the beginning of our love affair with the Dark Continent.*

We initially planned to go to Africa every other year, but after our 1998 buffalo hunt in Zimbabwe, we changed our minds and started taking a trip every year. Today, in 2008, I have been back every year but one, and I have hunted in Tanzania, Namibia (twice), and South Africa (five times). I have taken over fifty trophy animals, including four of the Big Five (I darted my rhino), and most of the small African antelopes. Space is too limited here to relate the story of even one stalk, but each lives in my memory, my diaries, and occasionally on film. I hope to finish my African collection before my legs give out.

Why do I do it? First of all, without trophy hunting, these animals would lose their economic value and be killed for food or because they endanger domestic animals or crops. Second, it is necessary to balance the population of the wildlife with its habitat, and, third, developing countries depend on hunting-related revenue as a major source of foreign currency. The hunting industry surprisingly produces much more revenue than wildlife tourism and comes with a smaller environmental footprint and lower impact on the land. In RSA and Namibia, farmers are forming conservancies and reintroducing animals that have not been seen in their areas for nearly a century. It is all about the animals, and, without the animals, it would not be Africa.

GOLABCHI

I have always wondered why I became interested in hunting. No one in my family, including my three brothers, is a hunter. From childhood I have always been fascinated with the outdoors and nature, and with mountains in particular. In the summer as a teenager, some friends and I would pack up and leave on foot for the mountains, where we would stay two or three days. We spent our time discovering new areas, and we did it without a tent, proper food, or clothing, but we had fun. When I was indoors, the biggest rooms were too small, and I felt as if the walls were pushing against me and suffocating me. Even today after a couple hours in the office and behind a desk, I need to get out.

When I am in the mountains, I feel at peace and closer to my Creator. Although these days I am no longer a spring chicken, I still love the mountains even more than before. Perhaps it's because at age sixty-seven each trip in the mountains means I am getting closer to my last climb. Of course, it would be sensible at my age to give up mountain climbing and hunting, but I intend to keep going. Every time I get back home, I begin to look forward to the next trip. I have been to all the mountain ranges in the world at least once, but to a majority of them I've been more than once.

Being in love with the mountains did not stop me from going into the deserts, swamps, and savannas, however. So far, I have made eighteen trips to Africa. It is true that I love my sheep and goats, but to me every animal deserves respect. I believe every animal is beautiful. When I am not hunting, I try to spend time in my trophy room, either with friends or alone. I am very proud of my achievements.

My first trophy room was built in 1982 and had 1,000 square feet; it was full by 1985. I added an additional 2,000 square feet and a high ceiling, and when it was finished, I thought that I would never be able to fill this room. But in 1990 I added another 4,000 square feet. Today this room is 7,000 square feet, and I have no space left either on the walls or the floor, and I am still hunting just as much. I have about 400 animals and over 250 species, and some are world records.

I have decided to donate my trophies to a museum or university for future generations to enjoy. I feel blessed to have been able to do what I love most, and I have always been thankful to the good Lord for providing me with this opportunity. It is my belief that the donation of my trophies to the public is a small price to pay for what the Lord has given me.

HENRIJEAN

Jacques Henrijean learned to shoot at the age of eight when he spent two or three hours a day motionless in fruit trees to prevent birds from taking the family's fruit during the tough days of World War II when all food was rationed. As a young man in the 1950s, Jacques worked at Lloyd's of London with the expectation of opening an office of his family's insurance business in Britain's capital. Unfortunately, Jacques was forced to return to Belgium on the untimely death of his father and to take over the reins of the family business.

Jacques insured some of the first Toyota cars imported into Europe from Japan, beginning with five or six cars per shipment, growing to nearly forty-eight thousand a year for Belgium within the first decade. To relax, Jacques went bird shooting. He quickly became a keen clay pigeon shot and won the Belgian championship five times. He was part of the Olympic Elite Skeet Team, and he has held the national record for Belgium in skeet (198/2000) since 1966.

After the International World Exhibition in Brussels in 1958, Jacques was asked to join a colleague on a chamois hunt near Garmisch Partenkirchen. The excitement of this trip encouraged Jacques to take up wild boar shooting; his interest in sheep trophies began with the acquisition of a Stone sheep in British Columbia in 1970. Jacques's first expedition to Africa was in 1972 where he took a black rhino close to the Tsavo National Park, Kenya.

When Micheline met Jacques, she had never even handled a rifle! Micheline grew up in Switzerland as a tomboy–hiking, skiing, and sailing with her three brothers. When the two met, she was an established and successful businesswoman involved in her own real estate company and the mother of two children. They met during a trip to the U.S.A. to witness the launch of Apollo 11.

The Henrijeans have always hunted together as a couple, and their safaris after exotic game started just before their wedding in 1971 when Jacques asked Micheline to accompany him to British Columbia for a mountain game hunt. He wanted to make sure that she was up to the job; she passed the test with flying colors.

During their honeymoon at the Royal Reserve near Tehran, both Jacques and Micheline were able to shoot rams from the same herd of Alborz red sheep. They also visited the Khosh-Yeilagh Wildlife Reserve to take a Trans-Caspian urial. This and subsequent visits to various parts of that enormous country ensured the acquisition of many excellent trophies, including specimens of urial, Armenian, red, Shiraz, and Laristan sheep. In 1973 they were back for Esfahan sheep, and in 1976 for a Kerman hybrid that they acquired close to the Persian Gulf. Some years later they were to experience the exotic lands of the Gobi Desert of Mongolia (around 1976) and then the Altai Mountains.

BROWN BEAR

Micheline insists hunting should not be considered an exclusively male sport. She relies on her deep motivation and commitment to hunting and to a stoical acceptance of all the discomforts that go with it. Micheline and Jacques declare themselves both fortunate and privileged to have been able to live an unforgettable and exciting hunting life together.

In her sporting career, Micheline was able to bag one of the world's rarest species of sheep, the Kamchatka bighorn (Ovis nivicola nivicola), that inhabit the vast area from the Kamchatka Peninsula west to the Putorana Mountains in northwestern Siberia and into the high country close to the Arctic Circle. The specimen was taken in July 1990 and the full story appeared in an article in Sporting Classics *magazine, May/June 1992, pages 62–66 and 135.*

Micheline always loved hunting with Jacques and sharing experiences, and as a husband-and-wife team they proved unstoppable. They were at one time the first and only couple in the world to both be "Super Slammers." This means they both had acquired twelve major world sheep specimens, which involved some grueling expeditions to remote places, including the Russian Caucuses. Micheline actually bagged nineteen sheep species! Micheline had already tackled numerous dangerous precipices and gorges to take the "Grand Slam" (this requires four species of North American sheep) in 1983, and at that time Jacques had completed his second North American "Grand Slam." Also around that time, Jacques won the coveted Weatherby Big Game Trophy Award (1984).

One of the highlights of the Henrijean collection is the polar bear trophy taken by Micheline during a hunt not far from Resolute Bay (Northwest Territories). That hunt involved a trip of over 250 miles on the ice. In order to gain this specimen, Inuit guides provided handmade caribou-skin clothing for

COUGAR

the Henrijeans. Two dog teams and sleds were used during the whole hunt.

One of the Henrijeans' most memorable expeditions was in Afghanistan in 1974. The expedition involved exhausting hunts on yaks in the Pamirs, encompassing summits of around 5,000 meters (16,405 feet) and temperatures below a minus 28 to minus 30 degrees Celsius (minus 18 to minus 22 degrees Fahrenheit).

Micheline's Marco Polo sheep trophy took eight days of searching and tracking, but she was able to bag it the day before the trip ended.

Micheline Henrijean was the first woman in the world to collect a record-book Marco Polo sheep in the Afghan Pamirs; she also acquired the No. 3 world-record giant forest hog in Ethiopia and the world's No. 3 Peters duiker in Cameroon. Jacques and Micheline Henrijean both legally collected the African Big Five during the 1980s.

Before selling their beautiful home, Jacques and Micheline Henrijean lived a secluded existence close to the Forêt de Soignies in Belgium. Their trophy room was immediately next to their home, a semiseparated pavilion of the same style as their main house. Each structure had high ceilings with wooden beams; a high, open fireplace; and some 185 trophies. The majority of the remarkable big-game trophies shown in these pictures were taken by Micheline because Jacques donated 157 trophies in his own collection in 1986 to the Museum of National Sciences in Brussels (Institut Royal des Sciences Naturelles de Belgique).

In their travels together, Jacques and Micheline have gone on more than 150 hunts to six continents, assembling together a collection of some 240 species of game. Their focus has been on mountain game hunting, but they enjoyed any adventure that brought the two of them together to face difficult and challenging situations. Each specimen represents an exciting memory for both Jacques and Micheline.

DIPLOMA

HIDVEGI

Bela Hidvegi, an international hunter and businessman, was born in 1936 in the small Hungarian town of Nagyszénás. In 1956, at the age of twenty, he left Hungary where he was studying at the Agricultural Academy of Keszthely to continue his studies in England. He earned a degree in food engineering and lived abroad for many years. At the beginning of the 1970s, he started to work for a well-known American food company as their marketing director, and, at the same time, he began to build strong ties once again with the agricultural and food industries in his native Hungary. His name is closely associated with sweet corn agro-industrial production.

During this time he discovered the legendary English gun manufacturing companies, and through his connections he was able to purchase Purdey and Holland & Holland guns at very reasonable prices. He had these guns reconditioned by craftsmen and sold them for a profit during hunts that he organized in Hungary. This enabled him to start his own gun collection and to travel farther and farther afield to hunt.

He began his hunting career by pursuing small and big game in Spain, Austria, the Czech Republic, and Transylvania as well as in his native Hungary and in Great Britain, his second home. At the beginning of the 1990s, he took his first African safari, and he has never been able to break free from the spell of that continent. He returns yearly and often twice yearly to hunt his favorite species, especially the spiral-horned antelopes and the rain-forest animals.

His trips have taken him to the savannas of Tanzania, the mountainous wilderness of Ethiopia, the Lake Kariba region of Zimbabwe, the Zambezi Delta, the hot and humid rain forests of the Central African Republic and Cameroon, the grassy plains and bushlands of South Africa, and the marshes of Zambia.

In North America, he has trekked in Alaska as far as the Brooks Range, and he has tracked through the boundless wilderness of the Rocky Mountains and the far north.

In Asia he began his quest for big game in the snowy wilderness of the Pamirs at 19,685 feet (6,000 meters) and in the Altai Mountains in Mongolia. In Pakistan he hunted in the Hindu Kush, Karakoram, and the Himalayas for two months. Further hunts took him to Iran where few travelers venture and where he hunted various species of sheep.

During the second half of the 1980s, Hidvegi once again settled in Hungary and brought with him his unrivaled trophy collection, the souvenirs of his amazing hunting career. He has graciously made a gift of his collection to the Hungarian Natural History Museum, where it is on exhibition at the Helikon Castle Museum in Keszthely. His fantastic collection includes hundreds of trophies, with more then 170 coming from outside his hunts in Europe.

He has a number of unique trophies, including a large maned lion; the timid, elusive bongo; all three subspecies of sitatunga from deep in the African marshes; a rare bay duiker whose trophy, one decade later, is still a world record; a gold-medal mountain nyala; a giant eland; and a warthog with 18-inch tusks. He also has a huge alpine ibex, a giant forest hog, a Marco Polo ram with 62½-inch horns, a huge argali, and three subspecies of markhor. One of the trophies in the collection remains a world record while 25 others are listed in the top ten in Safari Club International's record book. His philosophy is that the trophy is the greatest reward for a hunter and can be compared to a gold medal in other sports.

His trophy collection spans the wildlife of six continents and contains more than 150 life-size pieces set in their authentic habitats. It is not just one of the world's richest and most attractive collections; it is also the collection of a seasoned hunter who takes seriously being a role model for the younger generation of new hunters. Hidvegi views his collection as a fine teaching tool for educators.

In 2007, Hidvegi was awarded SCI's most prestigious prize, the World Hunting Award Ring. In 2009 he was the recipient of Ovis Club's prestigious "Triple Slam" award. He is perhaps proudest of the latter award since to win this award one needs to take one of each of the North American sheep (Grand Slam); the same for the rest of the world's sheep (Ovis World Slam); and, finally, the world's goats (Capra World Slam). The three together comprise the Triple Grand Slam, and to date only about four European hunters have been able to accomplish this feat. To crown all these achievements, Hidvegi received the National Hunting Order of Hungary in 2009, the highest Hungarian award.

He has also twice been the recipient of one of the Carlo Caldesi awards, considered the top prize for international mountain hunters. His name is inextricably tied to the Hungarian branch of SCI as well as to his activities with Nimrod Safari *magazine. Hidvegi has published two books:* Hunting Dreams *and* As a Hunter on the Peaks. *He has also produced three films in DVD format:* I Had a Dream, My Mountain Hunts, *and a documentary film* From the Wild to the Museum.

·VADÁSZATI KIÁLLÍTÁS · HUNTING

JONES

Most of my core story can be easily found in the opening chapter of my book, One Man, One Rifle, One Land, so I won't repeat it for this work. I would say that I've been greatly blessed to have been a hunter practically all my life, and I have had some excellent mentors, as well as a very understanding companion in my wife, Linda. I hunted small game until I was in medical school, when I killed my first deer, which was a welcome addition to the meager fare on which we subsisted in those days. From that point I gradually made a transition to hunting mostly big game.

I have taken a methodical approach to my big-game hunting, though this initially came about as a result of fortuitous factors beyond my control. I had killed perhaps ten North American species with my only rifle, a Remington 700 in .30-06, before I decided to try to take all the North American species with that same firearm. I completed the task in December of 1998, and subsequently finished the book mentioned above. I feel deeply privileged to have had the opportunity to do the hunting and research necessary to write that book, since many have told me it is the most comprehensive work on the subject. All my North American trophies are kept in a separate log home designed specifically for them. We have had many, many thousands of school children come through to see these mounts.

My systematic nature emerged again when I did my first overseas hunt, for I set out with the idea in mind to take all the Eurasian species with one rifle. Remington Arms, in appreciation for the kind words in my book about my original Model 700, gave me a fine Model 700 chambered in 7mm Ultra Magnum. As of this writing, I have taken 66 species in 26 countries with that incredibly accurate weapon. My target is 72 species, after which I intend to complete Another Rifle, Another Land. It is shaping up to be the truly definitive work on Eurasian hunting. I believe I am already one of very few people to take over 100, free-ranging big-game species without hunting in Africa—perhaps the only one. Moreover, I have used only one rifle on this quest—just as I did on my North American quest. Considering the increasing difficulty of traveling with a firearm, it could be quite impossible to do this in the future.

My Eurasian species have their own addition to my trophy house. That add-on features two separate mountains, and the photos here lack the ten Eurasian trophies that are not yet back from the taxidermist. I am saving only one wall for African trophies. I plan to mount only the Big Five plus a few of the more difficult African animals, if I am blessed to hunt in Africa someday. Others will be European-style mounts consisting of only the skull and horns. I currently have no plans for a book on African hunting since that subject has been exceedingly well covered by other authors.

Of course, I give all credit to the Lord Jesus Christ for the good things that have come my way. By His grace I have achieved a little bit in hunting and writing; my talent, physical ability, income, family, and myriad things I tend to take for granted are all gifts from Him.

GRAY WOLF
(CANIS LUPUS)
ALASKA

DESERT MULE DEER
SONORA, MEXICO
COUES DEER
NEW MEXICO
AMERICAN ALLIGATOR
(ALLIGATOR MISSISSIPPIENSIS)
FLORIDA
JULY 1997

KOKEN

I began big-game hunting at age sixteen when my family moved to India. But it wasn't trophy hunting. Since the Hindus don't eat beef, there was no meat in the local markets for our table. If we wanted fresh meat, we had to hunt. This was not pleasure hunting. There were about fifty American families where we were stationed, but only four of them were hunters. The four, which included my dad and me, kept all the families in meat. We hunted at night with a spotlight, and our primary target was a large antelope called a nilgai.

In my later years, after I had accumulated enough resources, I began trophy hunting. This endeavor took me to Texas, Arizona, Alaska, and Hawaii in the United States; Alberta, British Columbia, and the Yukon Territory in Canada; India, China, Tajikistan, and Mongolia in Asia; and the Central African Republic, South Africa, and Tanzania in Africa. I have collected over sixty species and have had all but four made into full body, life-size mounts. The most exciting trophy to me is my high-altitude Himalayan brown bear from northern India, which I took in 1965 and is No. 1 in the SCI record book.

In 2003 I established a foundation that is the parent of the Southeast Alaska Museum of Natural History. All the mounts, with the exception of the Himalayan brown bear and the sailfish, have been donated to this museum. The primary purpose of the museum is for educational use by the local school district and other Alaska school districts. It is also open to any other group of young people.

There is no natural history museum or zoological garden in southeastern Alaska. The result is that many young people in Juneau and the rest of southeastern Alaska grow up never having had the opportunity to view firsthand many of the wild animals from other parts of the world. The mounts are not behind barriers of any kind, so the kids are cautioned not to touch. Most of the animals are free standing, but there are three scenes that have been created using two or more animals. There is a touchy-feely section where the kids can handle hides, horns, antlers, and skulls.

The mission of the museum is to further the knowledge and well being of our youth and the regional community. The goal of the parent foundation is to provide a meaningful facility for field trips of school classes and other groups to learn about wild animals native to other continents. It is a great experience to watch the kids interact with these animals. The favorite among young people is the zebra.

KRÄLING

Cordelia and I grew up in different areas of Germany, but already in our childhood we were both in close contact with nature. Cordelia, born in the small town of Hagen, lived with her parents on an estate that had once been a working farm. I was born in the relatively large town of Dortmund in the Ruhrgebiet, but I grew up in a rural suburb and spent all my spare time on my grandparents' farm. It was there that I got to know the animals I would come across at the beginning of my hunting career, namely deer, hare, fox, and wild boar. I took the German hunter's examination in 1980, which was when I also obtained my high school diploma.

It wasn't until nearly ten years later that Cordelia and I were able to lease our first hunting estate. The hunting area was approximately 1,200 acres and was situated in a low mountain range. It was there that we harvested our first serious roe deer and wild boar trophies. We began going to the hunting show in Dortmund, and it was there that we encountered hunting opportunities from both local hunting outfitters as well as those from overseas. After hunting black bears, moose, stags, and European bison in Canada, Poland, and Lithuania, we decided that in addition to the hunt itself, it is also the trophy and, most important, the journey, that lures us. We feel it is a great privilege to experience the hunt together.

In the meantime we have learned what a special pleasure it is to share information about our hunting trips with other interested parties. This is why we were delighted to accept requests from different hunting magazines, including the renowned German hunting magazine Wild und Hund *and* Jagen Weltweit, *to publish reports once or twice a year. We found that our reports on the first leopard hunt using dogs in Namibia and on the "Small Vampires" of England (hunting for muntjac and Chinese water deer) proved very popular.*

In addition to the priceless memories of the hunts we've been on, we have collected over 150 species, which we display in a rustic environment. We've been on fifteen African safaris, two of which were self guided in Cameroon, for the important species of Central and Southern Africa, including the spiral-horn family. On hunts to Asia and North America, we were fortunate to bag exceptional trophies, including all the large cats, all the bears (polar, black, brown, Kodiak, grizzly, European brown bear), and all the wild oxen indigenous to those continents.

We live in a 250-year-old farmhouse, constructed mainly from natural quarry stone, where we house a part of our trophy collection. Some of our trophies from North America and Europe are now housed in our hunting chalet, which is situated close to our hunting area in the Sauerland. We still have space available to add to our collection, and we hope there will be time and opportunity to continue our passion of hunting the great game fields of the world together.

LAPINSKY

King Solomon's Mines, Trader Horn, The Snows of Kilimanjaro, and *Harry Black and the Tiger* are timeless masterpieces of African and Asian adventure. How could any normal man resist the chance to partake in the possibility of similar exploits? Tell me, how could any red-blooded American boy not be seduced by the siren song evoked by the thrill of the chase or by the exploration of the unknown? Well, I say, typical mortal flesh and psyche cannot help but be drawn to and intrigued by the allure of the world's wildest places . . . of big game, indigenous peoples, wild rivers, towering waterfalls, lush jungles, vast deserts, and mountaintop panoramas. Gratefully, there still exists an outlet for us hopeless romantics who, truly, just love to take our favorite rifles with us on faraway sporting holidays. When I talk of these romantic hunting sojourns, I am, of course, speaking of safaris.

Done correctly, while retaining the balanced attitude that nothing is certain in fair chase, a safari, whether in Alaska or Zimbabwe, South America or Asia, is simply a most wonderful opportunity as well as a tantalizing experience. Any experience distilled to its very essence can be considered a "little lifetime" where one first crawls, then walks, and finally takes off running. It's an experience where one may have some or all of his assets and deficits challenged by circumstance. Terrain, weather, disease or injury, native politics, unpredictable animals, and the fact that you are often more an observer of events as they unfold can stretch to the limit your ability to adapt.

You may win that 60-inch kudu or you may fumble the ball and don't get a shot on a 48-inch buffalo, but later bag a nice, heavily bossed 44-incher. *C'est la vie* . . . you're on safari and the hunt is still the same. A safari is one of the very few remaining honorable distractions available for the harried and overly civilized twenty-first century man—or, for that matter, any man, of any age in any time. Whether your kudu is 48 or 60 inches, or your buff is 38 or 48 inches, you're still a winner because you breathe the rarefied air of the chase, view stunning scenery, and interact with incredibly interesting creatures, often on a daily basis.

Big-game hunting has a way of concentrating one's mind while renewing one's spirit. It gives exercise to the limbs and eyes while generally making one feel more of that *élan vitale* than any half-dozen other forms of human pursuit. A safari demands this. And, you'll live most deeply and thoroughly. Your experience on safari will remain with you long after less glamorous ventures have deserted your memory.

For me, my trophy room possesses a *je ne sais quoi,* an indescribable something. It reenergizes those most cherished memories of times afield. It has been built around those things that trigger my enthusiasm for life. Big-game safaris have made that life more palpable for me. Sounds become clearer, colors are

brighter, and the air smells sweeter. Hunting, and reposing in the ambiance of my game room, makes my life better. And, it keeps me from getting confused! The safari forces an individual to sort out his priorities, and it allows him the opportunity to renew his acquaintance with his innermost self.

"Time is your ally, not your enemy." So you wait and postpone. However, "life is not a dress rehearsal; you only go around once"! So, you need to get "crackin." Clichés? Maybe. Nevertheless, your life on safari is one of the wisest uses of the time God allots to you, especially considering the rich dividends your body and soul will reap!

WILD
ABOUT

AMERICAN BLACK BEAR
ALASKA
BRONZE AWARD
ALASKA BROWN BEAR
ALASKA
BRONZE AWARD

LEWIS

People have trophy rooms for several reasons. Some have trophies to decorate their houses, and others have them to display special animals they have collected. But for me, my trophy room is there to help me relive the many special hunts I have taken over the years.

Many evenings as I sit alone in my very special room, I slowly gaze at one wall and then another. As I look at my trophies, I think about the hunts and the friends that each animal represents. I think about the time, for example, when I was out on the Alaskan Peninsula with my friend Gary LaRose Sr. on my first big-game hunt. It was raining outside and I was thinking, "Here I am, paying two hundred dollars a day to sit inside out of the rain, when I need to be outside hunting bear, moose, and caribou." (I was ultimately successful on all three and more.)

Then there was the time I took a Dall sheep with Joe Klutch, and I remember that we stood on the edge of an ice-cold mountain stream at midnight while I watched Joe standing in knee-deep water washing the blood out of the skin for a full-size mount. I think about my hunts with John Lucas Sr. and his great sons for polar bear, muskox, Arctic fox, and wolves, and how we froze out on the ice off Banks Island, Canada. I reflect on the many sheep hunts I took with great guides like George Kelly, Miles Bradford, and the guys in Baja working for the Mexican government.

Then I look at all the great trophies from Africa that I took with Geoff and Russ Broom. I think about Apio and Yolanda Reyneke and the great lions they guided me to. As though it were yesterday, I remember sitting in a camp in Botswana in 1972. The war was going full tilt in Southern Rhodesia, and the PHs, who were all Rhodesian, would each night sit and listen to the day's death count. Which family member, or neighbor, or friend had been killed that day? It was not a happy camp, but there were some great people. Game was plentiful back then, and the trophy fees were very low: lion $1,000, buffalo $150, elephant $800 plus ivory, crocodile $75, and leopard $600 . . . and that was for both the trophy and the license fee.

Zambia is special to me, for it was there that I got a great eland with Strung Middleton. I chased elephants with Wayne Dietrechsen in Zimbabwe, which was another great hunt. Nothing can top the great bushbucks and buffaloes I took with the super PHs at Jack Brittingham's Tanzania Adventures.

The world is a beautiful hunting ground and nothing is more beautiful than being in New Zealand and hunting chamois and tahr with Shane Quinn or Asian buffalo with Steve Fullerton in Australia.

Trophy rooms have special meanings to each hunter. To some it's the steep mountain in Alaska or British Columbia for a great bighorn sheep. To some it's the smell of the fire in the deer camp in South Texas. It can be sunsets in Africa or the dancing and singing of the natives when the hunters return to camp with a leopard or lion. As I look at each trophy and relive the hunt, I'm reminded of what hunting means to me.

PLEASE DO NOT TOUCH

PLEASE
DO NOT
TOUCH
PLEASE
DO NOT
TOUCH

PLEASE DO NOT TOUCH
PLEASE DO NOT TOUCH
PLEASE DO NOT TOUCH

PLEASE
DO NOT
TOUCH

MAYA
PLEASE
DO NOT
TOUCH

MÜLLER

Although I came from a family of nonhunters, I was born with a great love of animals and wildlife, which is still strong today. My hunting skills are of German origin, which are different from the ones in South Africa where I now live. Moving to South Africa and having a very successful business gave me the opportunity for great hunting. It is from this access to hunting that I have been able to acquire my trophies and build a beautiful room dedicated to them.

Hunting started for me seriously in 1974, and soon there was no space in our house for my trophies. I bought a farm surrounded by mountains near Johannesburg on the Crocodile River. It was there I planned to build a trophy room to highlight my hunting career.

I instructed the architect to design a magnificent home with the trophy room to be placed in the center. It was to be 21 feet, 4 inches (6.5 meters) high, surrounded by a tropical indoor garden. It also had to have a pond and a waterfall to supply moisture to the trophies because of our dry climate. It turned out just the way we wanted. Friends and visitors initially asked how I would ever fill that huge space, but today I am sorry it is not 50 percent larger.

The ceiling is made of solid meranti wood, as are the staircase and the bases of all the skull mounts, which I designed myself. The grouping of trophies is in no particular order with a few exceptions, like the European wall, the cats, and the desert animals. The red nyala bull has a prominent position, as only two have ever been hunted in South Africa. I particularly like dioramas, but I wanted to make sure that mine would be as natural as possible. I believe dioramas like the leopard catching a bushbuck and a male and female lynx ambushing a guinea fowl have brought life into my trophy room. When I sit quietly at my desk looking at my trophies, I am able to relive each hunt, which makes my trophy room all the more special for me. I think that only a hunter, perhaps, can understand what I am saying! (I must mention the taxidermist, whom I feel did exceptional quality work on my trophies. Thank you, Andre van Rooyen.)

Apart from our trophies, my wife and I are great lovers of live animals. We have fallow deer, nyalas, axis deer, and mouflon sheep on our property, and some are very tame. It goes without saying that none gets hunted!

NUÑEZ

A trophy room is mainly a place of dreams, a mirror where its owner revives the truth of each adventure that he exclusively knows. It is an environment where the author feels strong and weak at the same time.

When I designed my trophy room, I paid special attention to adding necessary warmth in every detail. For me, it was important to extend my feeling of closeness to each trophy in my room. To that end, I used thick planks of cork for half of the walls. For the other half, I used a realistic, but fake stone made of resin. I tried to mix both materials (cork and stone) in such a way so as to obtain breadth and to break up the monotony of any one medium.

The great fireplace is hung on a real stone base that comes from the Spanish Pyrenees. The same stone, specific to the area, covers the exterior of the house as well. The floor is made of a rustic Spanish ceramic tile, and under it, we installed a water heating system that invites walking barefoot on cold winter days.

We have installed a powerful home cinema with a big screen, which makes the viewing of a hunting DVD an experience nearly close to reality. The lighting system is multiple. Several halogen areas permit us to change the intensity of the light, helping us obtain an intimate atmosphere or maximum illumination. Since we live in Spain and the heat can be oppressive in summer, a good air conditioning system is necessary to maintain a stable cool temperature for the conservation of the trophies. The furniture is rustic and made of pine wood, except one area where computers and modern tables take their place. There is a centrally located billiard table, which gives snuff and brandy a special flavor.

I never counted the number of trophies I have, and I don't think I will ever do so. For me, the word "collection" takes shape and variety when it evokes memories of past adventures. I do not find big a difference between those animals considered to be "gold medal" and those considered only representative. In the end, they are all trophies, with each representing the same difficulty. I do not register trophies. The tiger that appears in the photos was never hunted, and it has a "CITES" certificate.

I believe that all species and every part of the world have their own attractiveness and interest, but I feel the most comfortable in the high mountains. Tajikistan, Kamchatka, Kyrgyzstan, Kazakhstan, Iran, the Balkans, Canada, and, logically, the European mountains have given me some unforgettable memories.

My trophy room has always been a secret place. Only a few good friends have broken its silence. It is a place that is alive and where I feel good. I believe that human life is changing fast and that we must count on the animals disappearing when the hunter does.

This particular volume of the Great Hunters *series will have a long shelf life, and it is for this reason that I open my trophy room to the public. I want my grandchildren and my great-great grandchildren to be reminded of what hunting was for me—a way of life.*

PANCOTTO*

Sam Pancotto was born in Chicago in 1927 to a family of nonhunters. There was no one in his family to instill in Sam an interest in hunting. His first tentative hunting experiences were for white-tailed deer in Wisconsin and Michigan. Instead of expanding his hunting adventures in North America as many hunters do, he remembers that he fell in love with Africa. He became "deathly sick" with the hunting fever in his desire to experience as much of the Dark Continent as possible. Then followed many years of long, multi-country safaris in the 1950s, 1960s, and 1970s. During those long-ago days, travel between African countries was easy and hassle-free. Safari costs were modest and bag limits were liberal.

A general license in almost every country allowed the hunter to take two elephants. Sam discovered his greatest hunting passion when he first trailed after the African elephant. He learned everything he could about elephants and elephant hunting, and he began to concentrate all his efforts on taking only the biggest bulls—those carrying tusks of a hundred pounds or more. Almost certainly, no safari client ever saw, tracked, and killed more hundred-pound bulls than Sam Pancotto. He shot an incredible nineteen hundred-pounders, a record unlikely ever to be broken. There were days when he literally kept his rifle case and a packed suitcase at the front door, ready to leave at a moment's notice upon the receipt of word of an enormous bull that had been spotted in any of several African countries.

He also fondly remembers the days of great hunting in North America—when Alaskan brown bear seasons were a hundred days long and when it was possible to take a polar bear and a brown bear on the same hunt. If a hunter wished, it was no great trick to collect a Grand Slam in three months with hunts in Alaska or the Yukon, British Columbia, Alberta, and Mexico. Hunters could and did take their rifles and ammunition onto commercial flights with them. Air travel was cheap, and red-tape and bureaucratic snarls between the United States and Canada and the United States and Mexico were nonexistent.

Other hunting passions for Sam were the great cats of Africa and the jaguar of South America. Besides cats, Sam also had a passion for wild sheep. His pursuit of North American sheep resulted in multiple Grand Slams, including one of the largest ever taken. He also hunted sheep in Asia, eventually collecting one of the largest High Altai argalis ever killed by a modern hunter.

On a different note, it was during the course of jaguar hunting in South America that Sam became aware of the desperate schooling needs for young children in British Honduras. And, ironically, it was not the squeeze of a trigger, but rather the stroke of a pen and the writing of one check that

**Written by Robert Anderson*

Sam & Rosemary Pancotto

made possible the creation of the Pancotto Primary School for young children. This just may be Sam Pancotto's finest trophy.

Today, Sam is somewhat wistful about the old days of international big-game hunting, but he is thankful that he was able to do what he did when it was still the golden age of safari hunting. Times have changed, and those days will likely never return. Sam has accumulated a veritable treasure chest of memories, which can be seen in his trophy collection.

PIERCE

My hunting career began in the early 1960s. Growing up surrounded by the hills around Oakland, California, I was limited to a pellet gun for rabbits and other small game. I went on my first big-game hunt for black-tailed deer with my father and uncle when I was eight. I have always loved the oak-studded foothills in Mendocino County for the pursuit of trophy black-tailed deer, and after all these years it is still my favorite hunting experience.

I joined FNAWS and SCI in 1980 and learned about all the great international hunting opportunities. New and wonderful adventures began for me, and in 1980 I shot my first Dall sheep. I completed my first Grand Slam in 1984. After being exposed to conservation groups like FNAWS and SCI, I traveled to Asia, and in 1996 I completed my ISHA Super-Slam. In the meantime I still continued to take lots of North American trips. In early 2000 my good friend, Ridge Taylor, talked me into a twenty-eight-day safari to Tanzania.

It soon became apparent that with all my North American and Asian hunts and with hunting seven straight years in Africa, I needed somewhere to display my trophies. This became a pressing issue for me. My trophy room would contain memorabilia of my hunting lifestyle as well as be a tribute to the animals I've hunted and the countries I've visited. In 2003 I located a piece of property in California where I designed and built a new home with an attached trophy room.

It's been my good fortune to have collected these wonderful trophies, so I wanted a hunting theme to be carried throughout my home. My trophy room contains dioramas, and care was taken to make these as realistic as possible. The back wall in my room is a sheep mountain with fifty-five life-size sheep, goats, and ibexes. The right wall contains trophies from North America, and the left wall has all African trophies. The centerpiece is an African tree, surrounded by my African trophies. The bar area contains shoulder mounts and a gun display.

John Lewton was the designer and did the animal placement, and Animal Artistry and McKennas's Wildlife Designs did the majority of the taxidermy. To create a realistic habitat, I used reproduction bald eagles, owls, and reptiles as finishing touches. I'm not done yet, as I am packing my Bansner rifle to head up north to hunt that wily trophy, the black-tailed deer, again.

When one enters my trophy room, it reflects the wild places I've been to and pays tribute to the animals I've harvested. The atmosphere is perfect for recounting tales of past and future hunts, like the two trips I made by dogsled in the Arctic. I was in pursuit of a polar bear, and I finally succeeded on the second trip . . . after sixty, long, cold days! Those were my most humbling experiences.

I would like to give thanks to everyone involved in my hunting career (guides, outfitters, booking agents) and especially to my dad and uncle for getting me started pursuing game at a young age. Conservation groups like SCI, FNAWS, and Ovis will help ensure the opportunity for others to be able to follow my path.

Great Hunters

NO
HUNTING

PROTHERO

I don't have a trophy room, I have four of them—great rooms ranging from 600 to 1,000 square feet, all with vaulted ceilings, skylights, and lots of wood. I take pride in the wood floors throughout; the ceilings and all but one wall is wood, too—pine, cedar, fir, and redwood. Skylights and natural light show off game mounts as no artificial light can. Each room has its own theme. The North American Room contains forty or so North American trophies, the African Room has the same number of African game mounts, and the Boreal Room contains only trophies from the northern hemisphere. In the Boreal Room reside most of my sheep and goats, including the Grand and World Slams, for whatever that is worth, and at least half of the full-body bear mounts. You get the picture.

The house is more than a trophy repository. I've collected handmade carpets from Anatolia, Azerbaijan, Turkmenistan, Baluchistan, China, and Navajoland; basketry from aboriginal North America and every sub-Saharan African country in which we've hunted; and aboriginal musical instruments, spears, swords, daggers, textiles, carvings, artifacts, and art from all over Africa, Siberia, the Russian Far East, Mongolia, Nunavut, Canada, Mexico, and China.

The house is a work in progress. I started building it three decades ago. It's of log construction, and it's still evolving, though I like to think we've added the last wing and room. I've done almost all the work myself, too, though Cheri did the wiring (she's an electrical contractor), and I had help with the plumbing.

The house is located in the Nordic Valley Ski area in northern Utah at 6,000 feet in elevation. It is the wettest locale in the state. Last winter we had 77 inches of snow on the ground, but it's heavily wooded and surrounded by mountains, and in summer it's spectacular. Fortunately, we seldom get that much snow.

I prefer hunting mountain sheep to any other animal because it's mostly a fair-chase proposition. Seldom can you drive to the locale, gadgetry plays less of a role, and you work for what you get. Ibex are as much fun because of the tougher terrain. Finger-and-toeing ibex geography often gives an adrenaline rush more powerful than a charge from a Cape buffalo.

I'd guess my toughest hunt, though, was after polar bear by dogsled on Arctic Ocean pack ice in the full winter of early March, mainly because of the intense cold. It never got above 30 below zero! We camped in wall tents and endured 50-knot gales, bears in camp, and getting lost for the best part of two weeks before I finally collected a 10-foot bear, perhaps my most valued trophy. We hunted

Marco Polo sheep in December at 16,000 feet in Tajikistan's Pamirs in temps down to 25 below, and I value my 62x17-inch ram nearly as much as the polar bear. My African lion, top-5-class Dagestan tur, Eurasian boar, Hangai argali, leopards, and largest mule deer bucks rank right up there, too.

Cheri was right there for most of it, and she out-toughed us all.

SAFARI

RIGOTTI

In 2007 my wife and I traveled to Spain for hunting and pleasure, and while there we saw many grand and elegant Mediterranean homes. On the airplane home, we decided to build our dream home, and we resolved to base our concept on the grandeur and elegance of the homes we had seen in Spain. Lori Magel of Lori Magel Homes and my wife, Yvonne, designed and decorated our new home.

The house is 5,400 square feet on half an acre overlooking the fairway of a golf course. Massive stone columns connect the arches in front and back of this U-shaped house. Within the U lies a 20x40-foot custom pool with an 8-person hot tub incorporated within the pool. Throughout our home are 12-foot ceilings with 8-foot doors and 11-foot arches. The floors are hardwood, and there are four fireplaces to give a warm feeling to our home. The grounds are beautifully landscaped, there is a circular driveway, and slate paths wind through palm trees. Plants were specifically chosen to give an illusion of a Mediterranean setting. Artist Rick Taylor did my first ram in bronze, and we have it perched on a rock in our garden.

The trophy room is 40 feet by 30 feet with rustic barn wood, beam ceiling, and a granite wet bar. The fireplace and lighting set off this warm, natural, and cozy atmosphere. Bronze sculptures by Rick Taylor are displayed in the trophy room and the office. Pictures of all the trophies hang on the entry wall to the trophy room, and each picture has an engraved plaque stating the date, country, and species of the animal. Brian Samuel, a local taxidermist, mounted most of the trophies seen on these pages.

In 1991, I drew a once-in-a-lifetime sheep tag in Oregon. I hunted in the Steens Mountains for a California bighorn. I shot my ram at 10,000 feet on the last day, two hours before dark, and from that day forward, I have had what's called **sheep fever!** I love the challenge of climbing the mountains where these majestic animals live. I have taken the North American Grand Slam (Dall, Stone, Rocky Mountain, California, and desert bighorn sheep); the Ovis World Slam of thirty-three species of sheep; and the Capra World Slam of twenty-four species of goats. Hunting these animals has taken me to the far mountains of Pakistan, Azerbaijan, Kyrgyzstan, Uzbekistan, Tajikistan, Turkmenistan, Mongolia, China, Russia, Siberia, Turkey, Spain, Switzerland, Bulgaria, Romania, Hungary, New Zealand, Hawaii, and, of course, throughout the continent of North America.

Traveling and hunting in exotic destinations is only one part of the adventure. For me, meeting the people, living and learning about their cultures, and seeing their way of life have enriched my own life. I have discovered that people are people wherever they live, and I have made many new friends on my travels. One of these new friends is Larry Higgins from Michigan, and sharing camps with this man has truly been a pleasure for me. My hunts have provided me with many great memories that will last a lifetime.

HIMALAYAS
ROCKIES

Gary & Yvonne Rigotti

SPANISH
CONQUEST

SODIRO

I believe my passion for hunting began the same day I was born, for it is something I've got under my skin, flowing in my veins, making me shiver out of emotion each day of my life. My first weapon was a small shotgun, in caliber .410, with which at the age of seven or eight I chased hares, partridges, and occasionally ducks on our family grounds in the center of Santa Fe, a province of my beloved Argentina.

My first big-game trophy was a brocket deer—a female to my eternal shame! I went on my first safari in 1967 to Uganda and Rwanda, and it was typical of the hunts offered at the time: the hunt lasted 45 days and was exorbitantly priced at U.S. $80 a day! It was a safari to remember, and it meant everything to me, filling me with emotion, madness, and passion. I think it taught me to love and respect animals, and to appreciate them in their purity and magnificence as part of the whole work of an infinitely superior being. I learned to love them so much that I firmly promised myself never to hunt more than one specimen of each species. I've definitely kept that promise all my life, with the exception of the most common species that I shoot for food.

The Lord, in His incredible kindness, has granted me the resources to hunt throughout six of the seven continents. I have hunted in deserts under a burning sun, in tropical forests, on plains, and in the mountains at 17,000 feet. I have hunted at temperatures of minus 40 degrees Celsius (minus 40 degrees Fahrenheit) as well as in boiling weather. I walked around many countries, leaving part of my life in each. I cherish unforgettable memories from them all, but none of them has reached so deeply inside me as the wonderful continent of Africa.

My trophy room is today an open museum with 277 species displayed. There are almost 30 more at the taxidermists both in Africa and in Argentina. I'm proud of owning a whole collection of every South American prey. I have all the big-game trophies from North America except for a tule elk, which is my target for this year, and I have almost all from Europe, all from Oceania, many from Asia, and 123 from Africa.

As far as I know, I am the only living hunter who has been fortunate enough to hunt tigers in India legally. They, together with my bongo, sable antelope (the most beautiful antelope of the world), and sitatungas, are the trophies that give me the greatest satisfaction.

Obviously, my collection and my modest achievements are not exclusively mine, but they also belong to my dear wife and my children who forgave my long absences, understood me, and supported me. A very important part also belongs to my outfitters and those who have accompanied and helped me in my adventures.

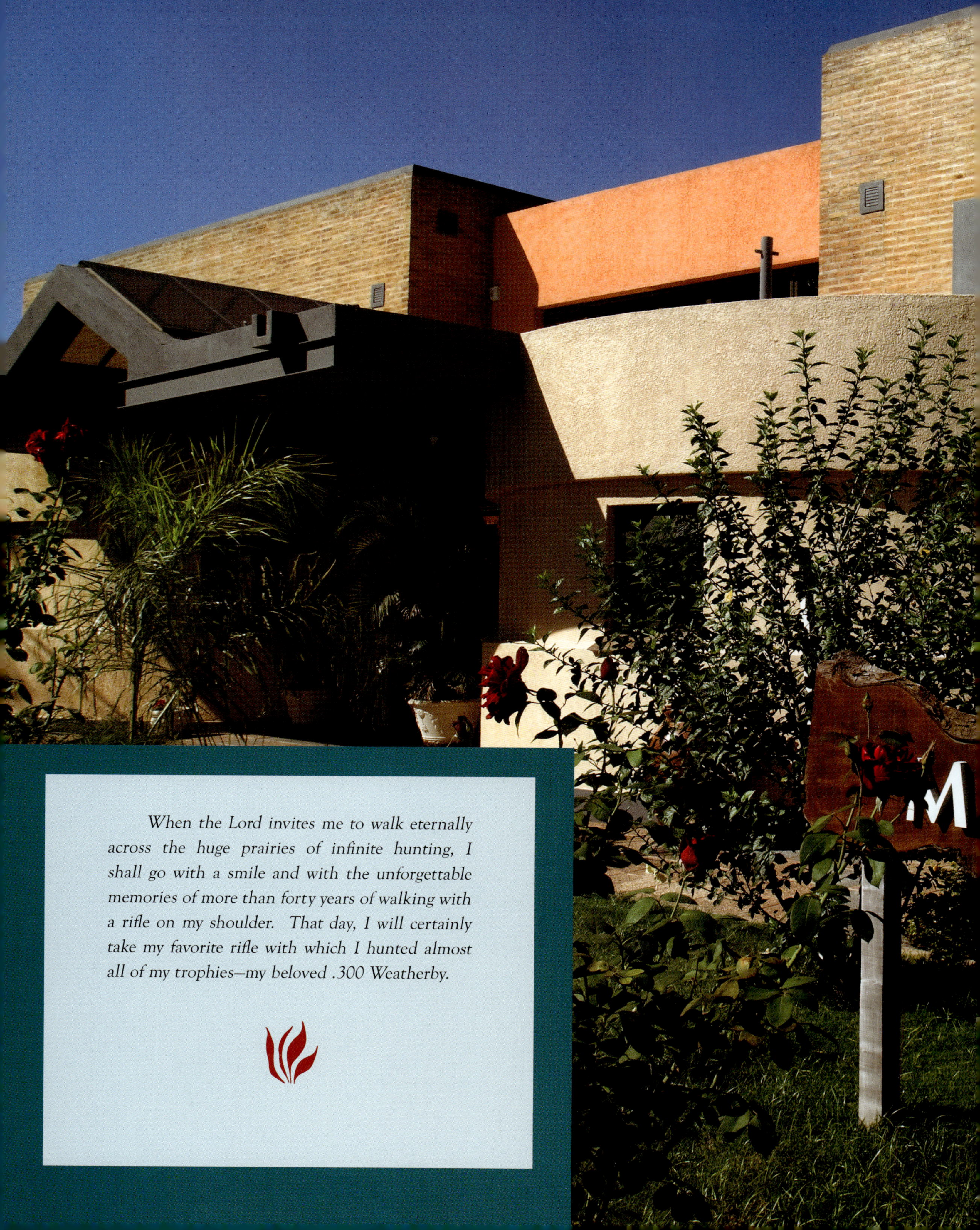

When the Lord invites me to walk eternally across the huge prairies of infinite hunting, I shall go with a smile and with the unforgettable memories of more than forty years of walking with a rifle on my shoulder. That day, I will certainly take my favorite rifle with which I hunted almost all of my trophies—my beloved .300 Weatherby.

SEO DE CAZA

No os podeis quejar de mi,
si buena vida os quité, mejor
NO TOCAR

ANTILOPE NEGRO
(India)
AS.18

DE VILLIERS

I am an only son of a single mother, and though we were poor, my mother never complained. I always remember her saying that she would make sure that I would get a good education, and that education would be the key to my future. We lived in a one-bedroom flat in Hillbrow, a suburb of Johannesburg, South Africa. In the afternoons after school I would play in a vacant lot near our flat, and I always pretended to be a farmer, saying to myself that one day I would own a farm. This idea was forgotten for many years. I qualified as a doctor in 1973, and I worked for a few years before I took a break in 1976 to travel.

While in Spain, I would listen to the BBC news at night, so I heard about all the violence back in my hometown. I decided that when I returned home I would buy a handgun, but before buying the gun, I first wanted to do a bit of research. When I went to the bookstore, I quickly realized that people were hunting with handguns, and the more I read the more inspired I became over my new hobby. In no time I was a handgun fanatic, shooting combat with my Colt pistol and hunting with my Colt Python revolver.

I became a member of Handgun Hunters International and arranged handgun hunts for the president of SSK Industries, J. D. Jones. I met Larry Kelly and became a close friend to Mark Hampton, who has taken hundreds of SCI trophies with a handgun. By 1980 I owned twenty-two specialized hunting handguns and had hunted literally hundreds of animals, including a world-record white rhino, with a handgun. (My rhino would still be No. 1 in the SCI record book had I not sold it, so I could not have it remeasured.)

By 1982 my ears had become severely damaged by all the loud gunshots, and so my friend Barry Gordon, who at that time owned a bow shop in the Carlton Center in Johannesburg, convinced me just to "try" bow hunting. Compared to the massive kinetic energies my "hand cannons" produced, the bows were no match. I was totally convinced that it would be a disaster, but I promised Barry to give bow hunting my best shot. As they say in the classics, "The rest is history."

Once I realized that bows are, in fact, deadly weapons, I was hooked. I now no longer bragged about how long the shot was but how close I could get before I shot. What I liked the most was the fact that I was supplying all the energy to propel the arrow and that there was no loud explosion. With the correct equipment, any animal can be killed with a single arrow.

My first goal was to be the first South African to hunt the Big Five and the hippo with a bow and arrow. I also wanted to be the first person to shoot all the Big Six by "walk and stalk" and not over a bait or from a hide. I achieved this goal by 1992 when I was forty-four.

By 2009 I had hunted over one thousand animals on three continents. These were all hunts on foot, and they include twenty-six buffaloes (three species), three elephants, two leopards, and the Big Six.

I always enjoy reading *Safari* magazine to see what my old friend Mark Hampton is up to and then see what other new and interesting animals I can hunt. I enjoy choosing a category from SCI such as "wild oxen of the world" and then trying to hunt all of them. I now have only one left to complete this category.

My long-ago wish to own my own farm finally came about in the 1980s when I bought my first game farm. All the meat rations for the staff on my farm have been hunted with a bow and arrow, and that has allowed me to shoot well over one thousand animals up until now.

I probably have at least twenty top-ten animals that I still have to enter into the SCI record books. If I did not have the expense of running a game farm, I could not have thought of anything I would like to do more than emulating people like Chuck Adams, Steve Kobrine, Tom Miranda, Archie Nesbit, and all those other wealthy bow hunters who travel the world hunting exotic animals in really exotic places.

I usually don't bother to explain to nonhunters why I bow hunt, for it seems to me that people will hear what they want to hear. The bottom line, however, is that when hunting a specific species of animal it may take years of planning and paperwork as well as weeks of traveling and walking, whereas the act of shooting takes only a few seconds. We hunt for the whole experience, not just that final shot.

For the moment I am content watching my animals on our game farm on the Crocodile River, but if I win the lottery or get a sponsor I'll be booking a bongo or a giant forest hog safari in a flash. For the moment, I continue to be a professional hunter and outfitter, dangerous game bow hunter and guide, game-farm owner and game breeder, National Bowhunter Education Foundation master instructor, African Bowhunter Organization master instructor, member of the SCI African Bowhunter chapter, and SCI master measurer.

IMPALA
BUSHPIG
WARTHOG
WATERBUCK
DR ADRIAN DE VILLIERS

BUSHBUCK
BLESBUCK
PSE
BOWHUNTER
ASIAN

IMPALA
BUSHPIG

YURÉN

For me, hunting has been a way of life. My quest for game has taken me from the summits of Asian mountains to the lowest-lying deserts, and from the frozen ice fields of the North Pole to the rain forests of South America. In this search, I have collected 317 species, but, even more importantly, I have been in the most remote, secluded places anyone could imagine, coming into contact with the most authentic of all the inhabitants.

Wherever I have been, I have tried to sow love—love that I harvested in abundance during the thirty-nine years that the good Lord granted me with my beloved Pita. With her, I learned that, for the real sportsman, hunting is a form of passionate, reciprocal love between the hunter and his prey—a love so great that the prey yields up its life in order to become immortal. Prey and hunter merge at the moment of collection and never again separate, entering into a mystic, esoteric relationship whose nature is philosophical—an arcane, sacramental mystery that can be comprehended only by those who have been initiated into the liturgy of the hunt.

My trophy room is the concrete manifestation of this relationship, being a tribute to the beauty and poise of the game. The trophies that are preserved in this room reveal their beauty to those who have never had the privilege of admiring them in their native habitat, teaching us that hunting is necessary for real conservation. My old trophy room served me for more than thirty years, until there was no more space left in it to lodge the more than six hundred mounts that were the fruit of my lifelong passion.

Instead of building a house with a trophy room, I constructed a trophy room with bedrooms, thus embarking on the last part of my life in the hope of being able to continue planting and harvesting love. One day the good Lord will call me to pitch my tent in the happy hunting grounds. Until then, my mounts will remain in the sanctuary that I have built for them, showing their beauty to those who did not have the good fortune of seeing them while they were alive and taking their place in my immortal collection.

May the words of Don Juan, the memorable character created by the Spanish poet, José Zorrilla, serve to remind both my reader and myself, once again, that my trophy room is dedicated to the animals I have collected throughout my happy life. On the wall overlooking its main hall the visitor can read: "Those killed by me must not complain; if good life I took away, better grave I give today."

Villaraña, 12 July 2009

INRI

no os podéis quejar de mi, vosotros a quien maté,
si buena vida os quité, mejor sepultura os di

JESÚS YURÉN

SAFARI PRESS